MAZE

FOR KIDS

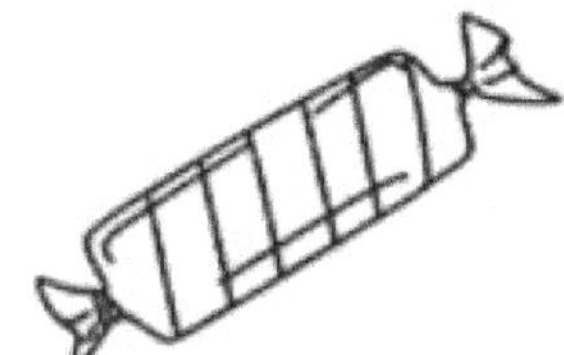

MAZE BOOK

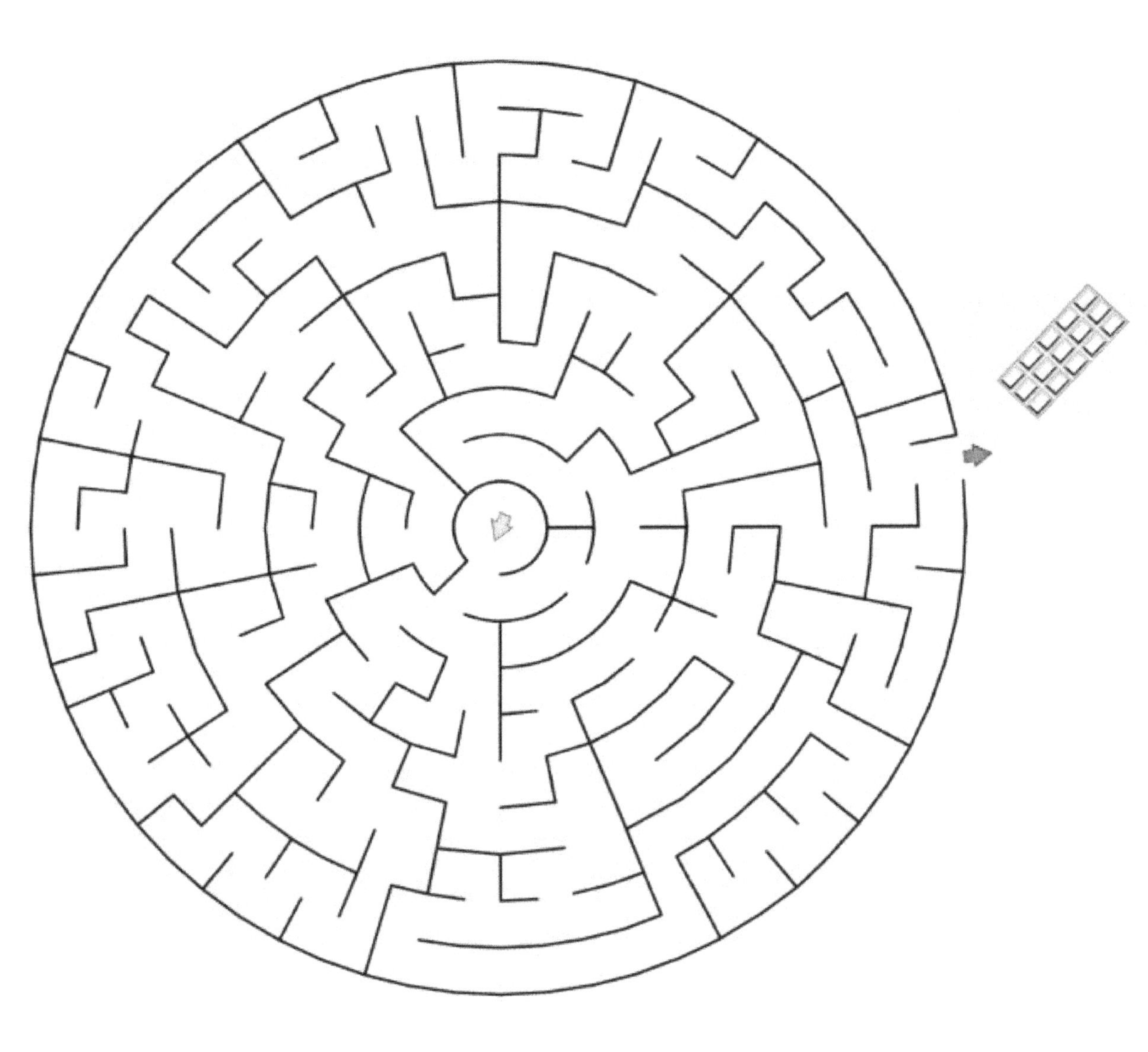

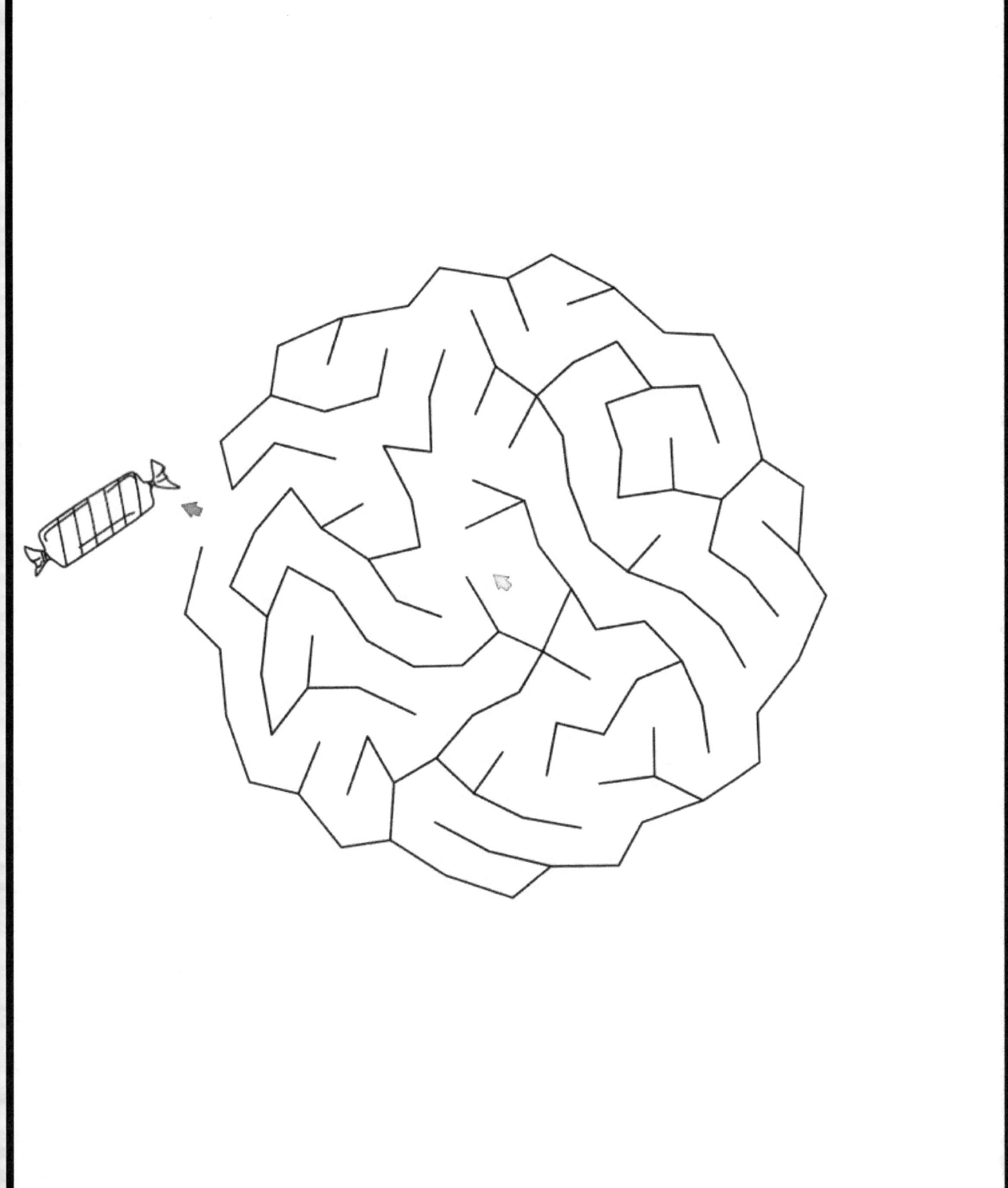

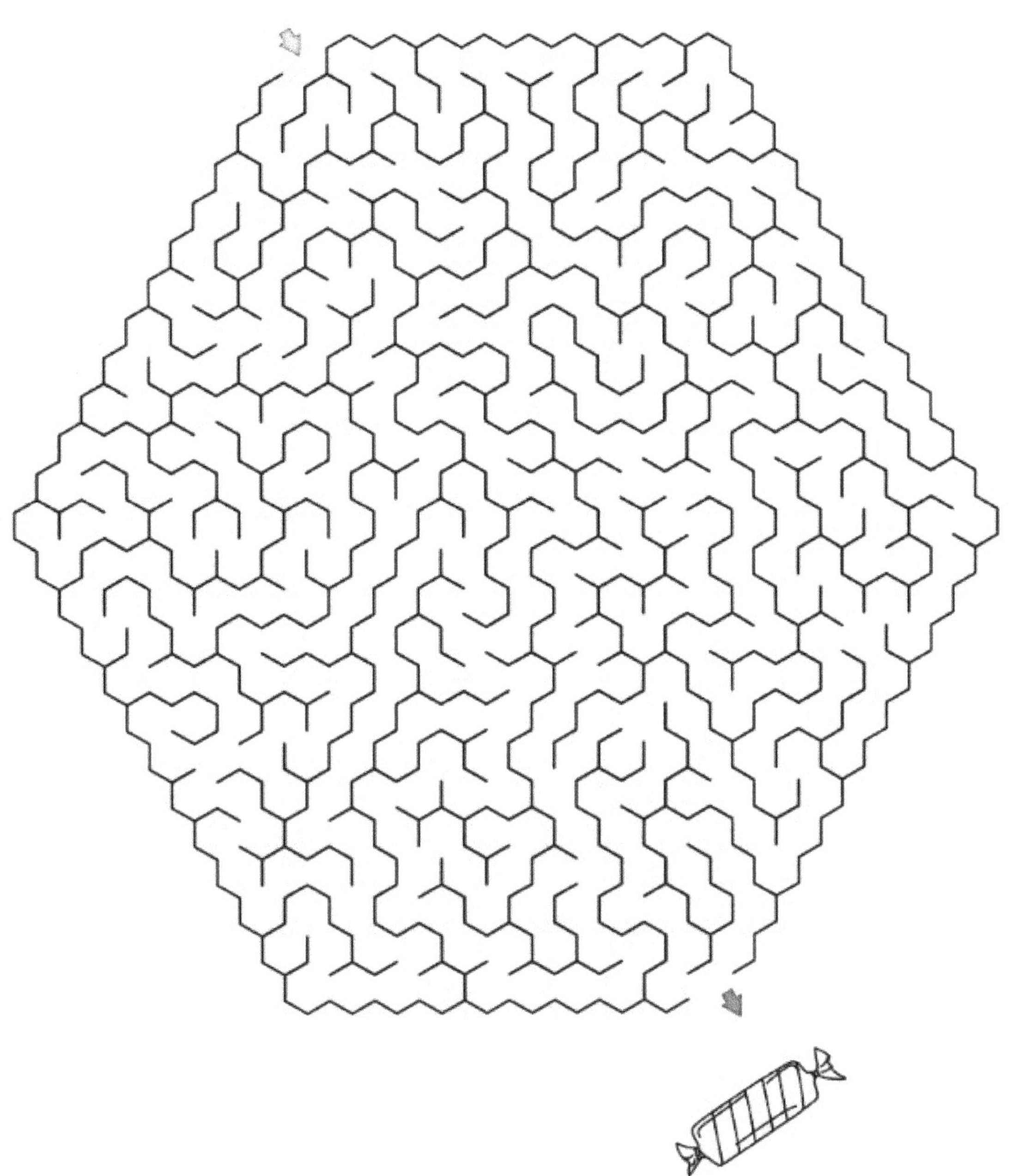

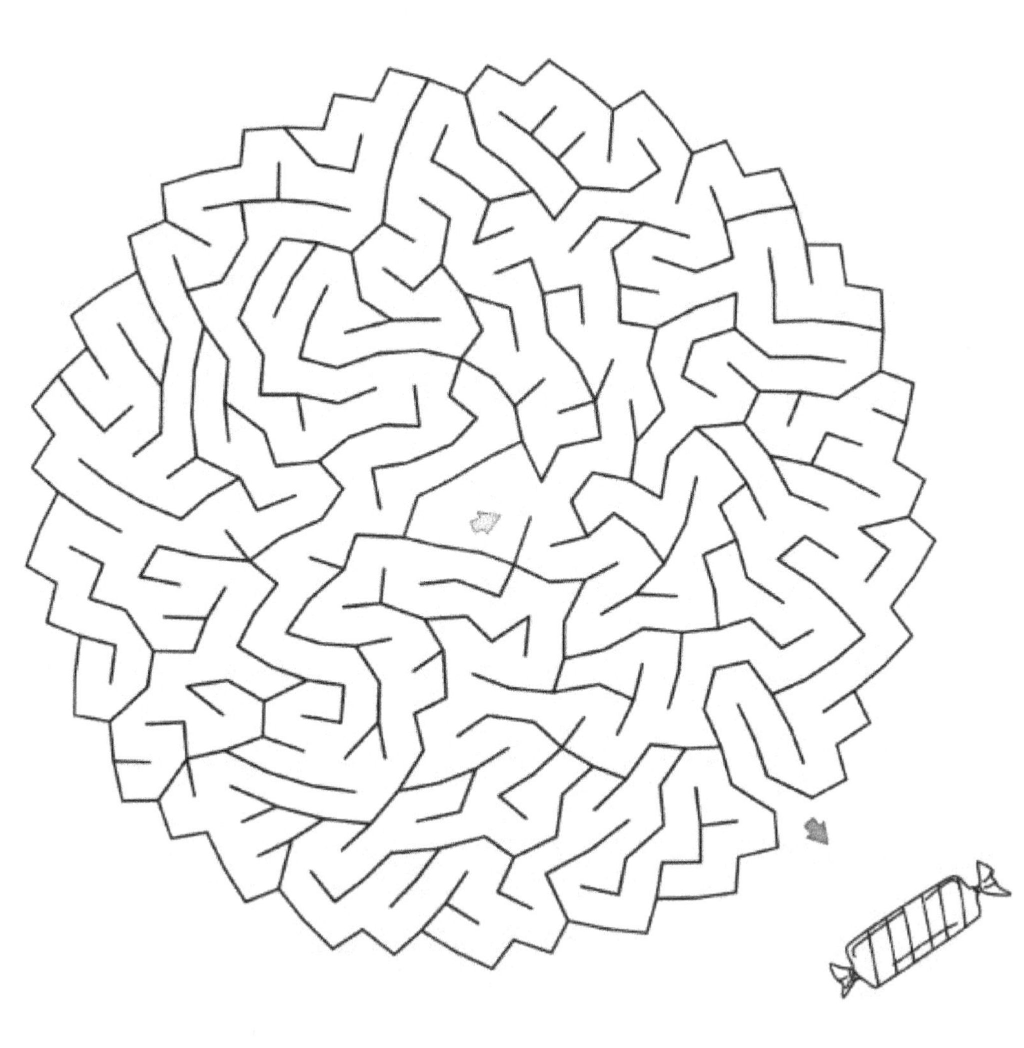

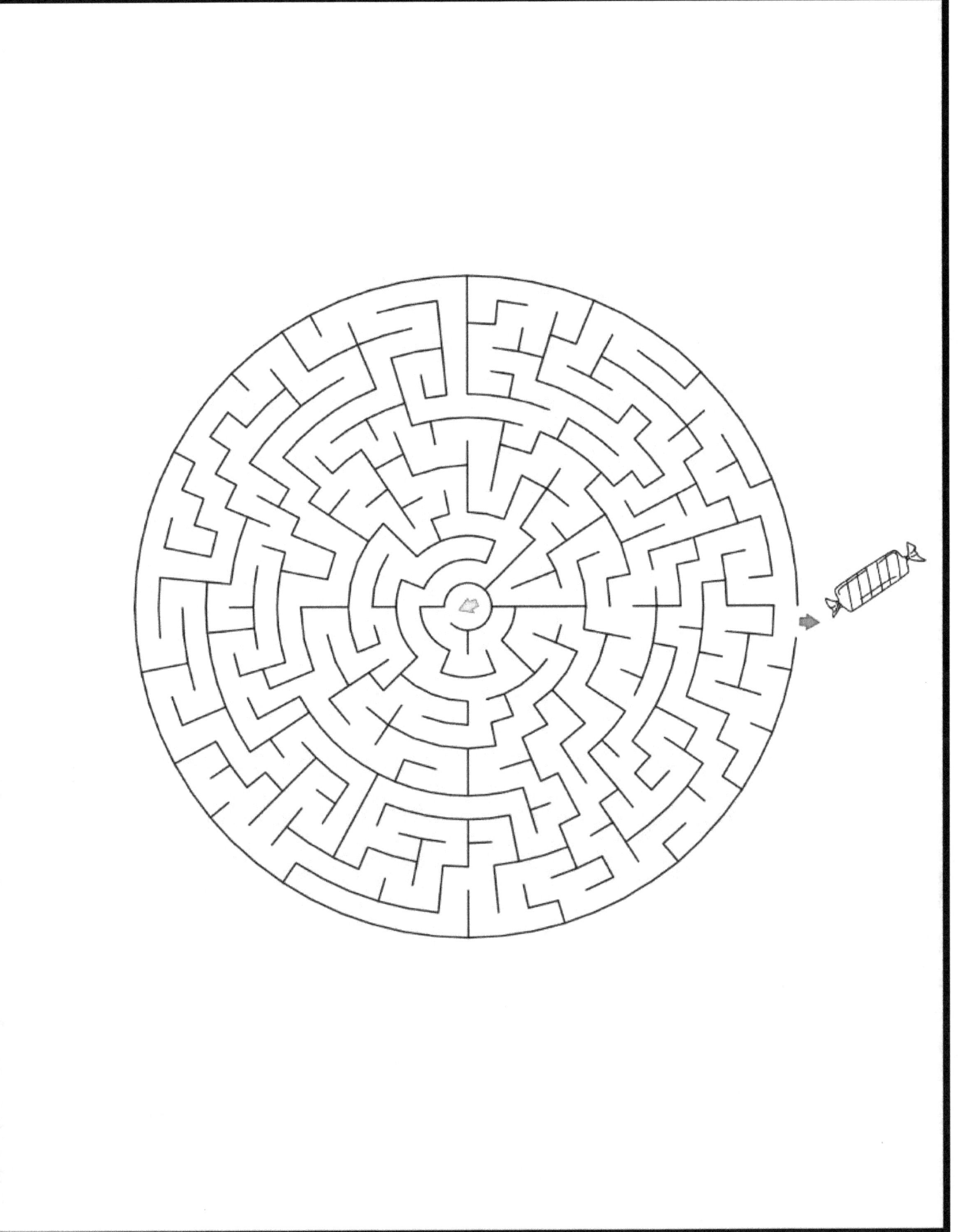

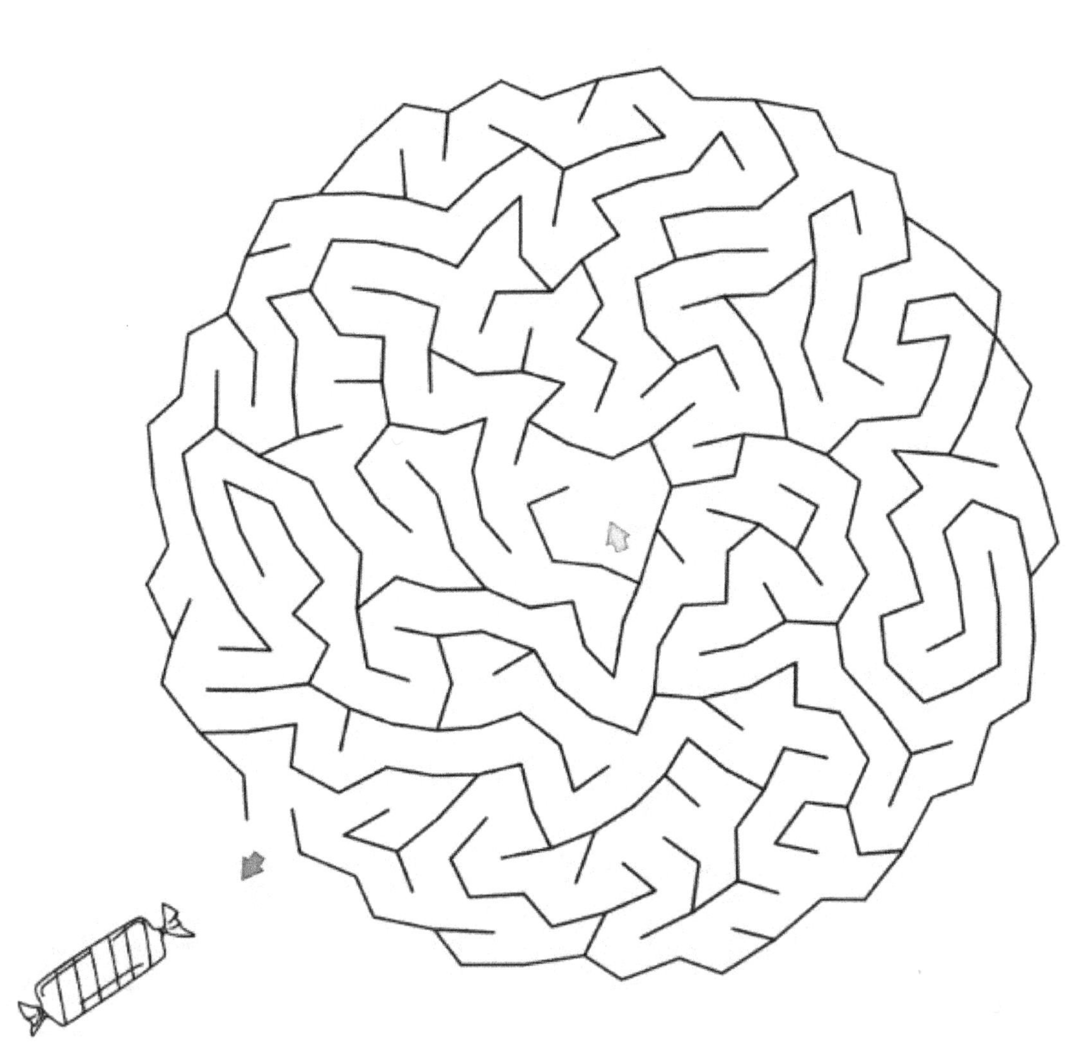

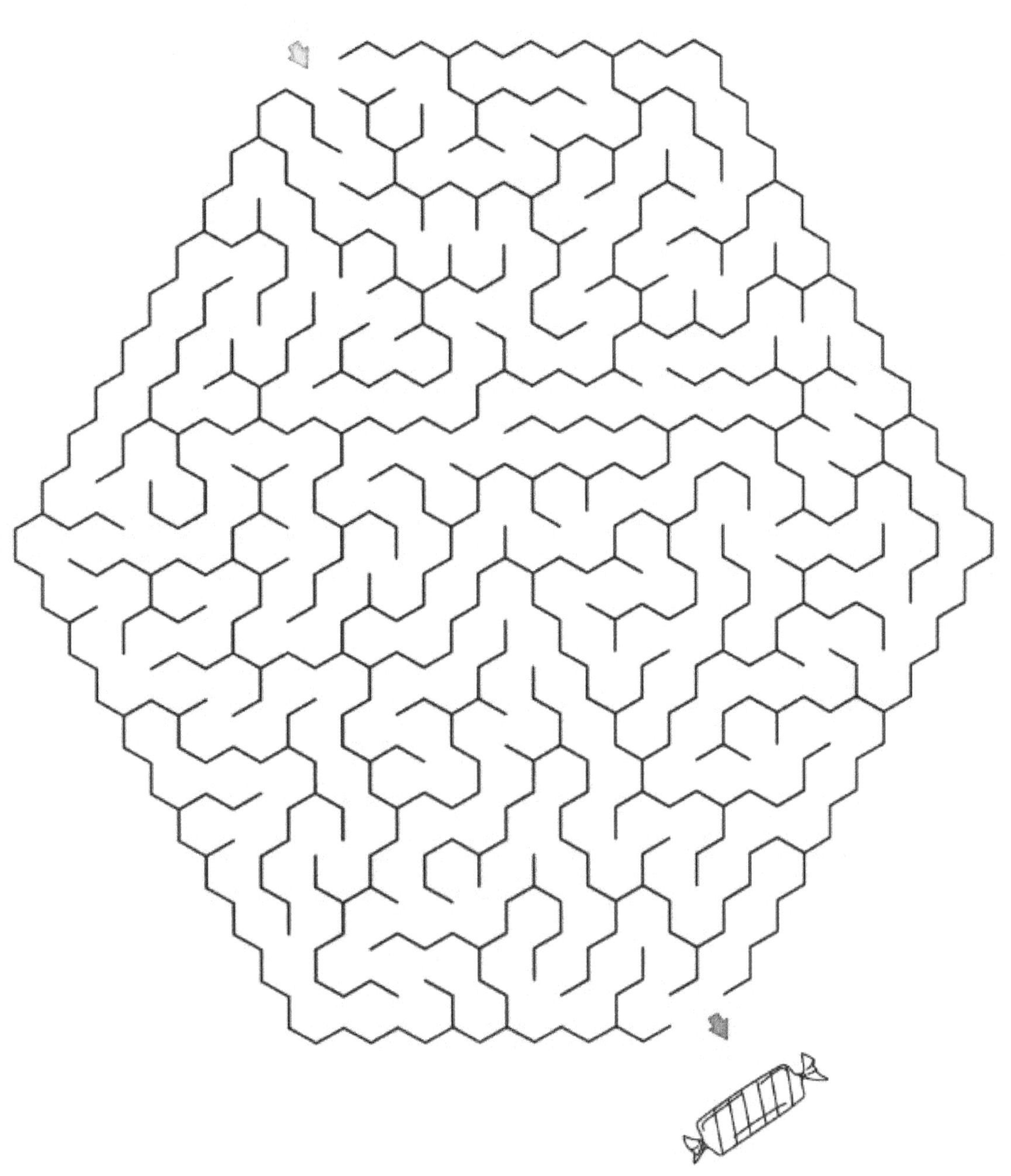

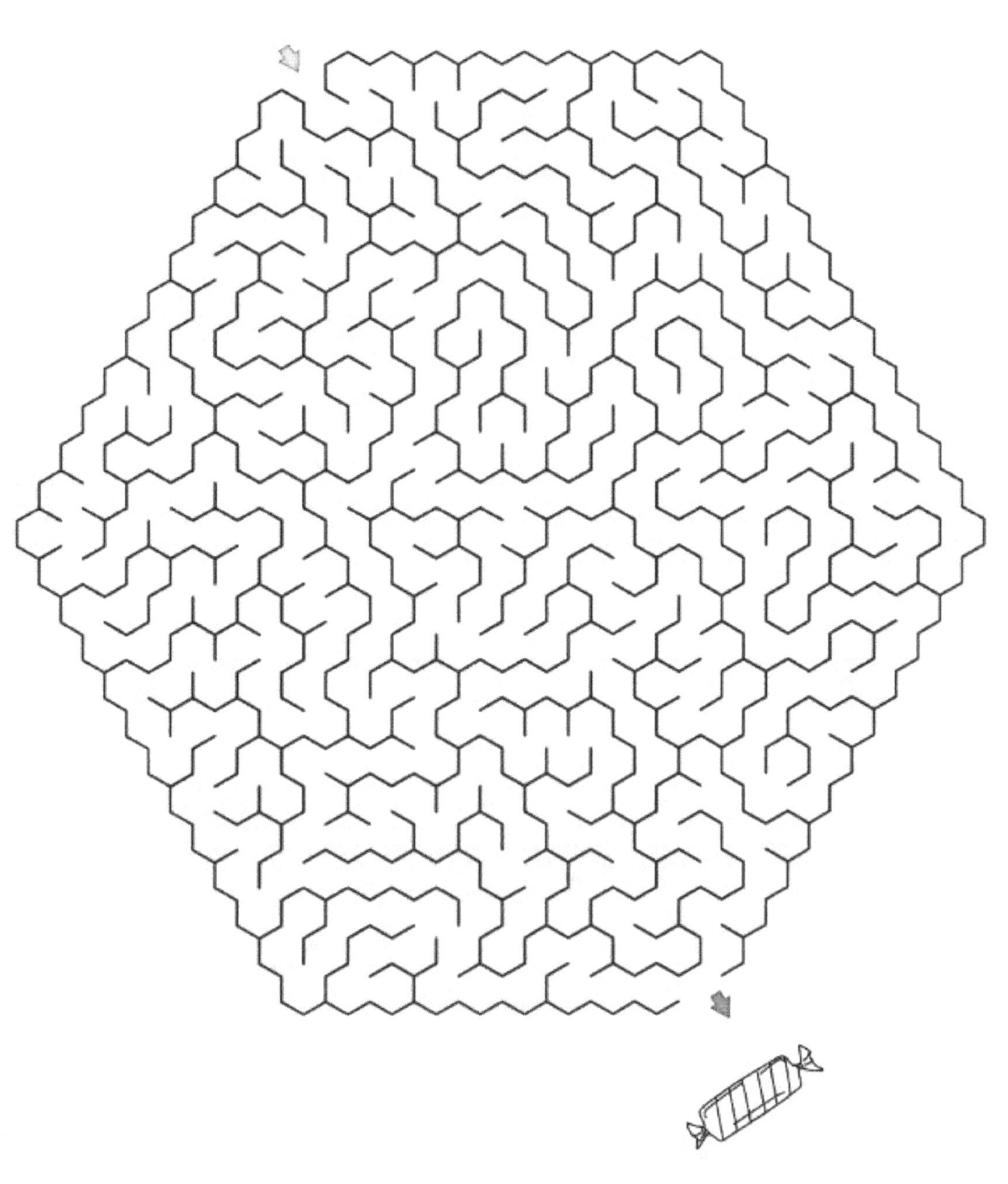

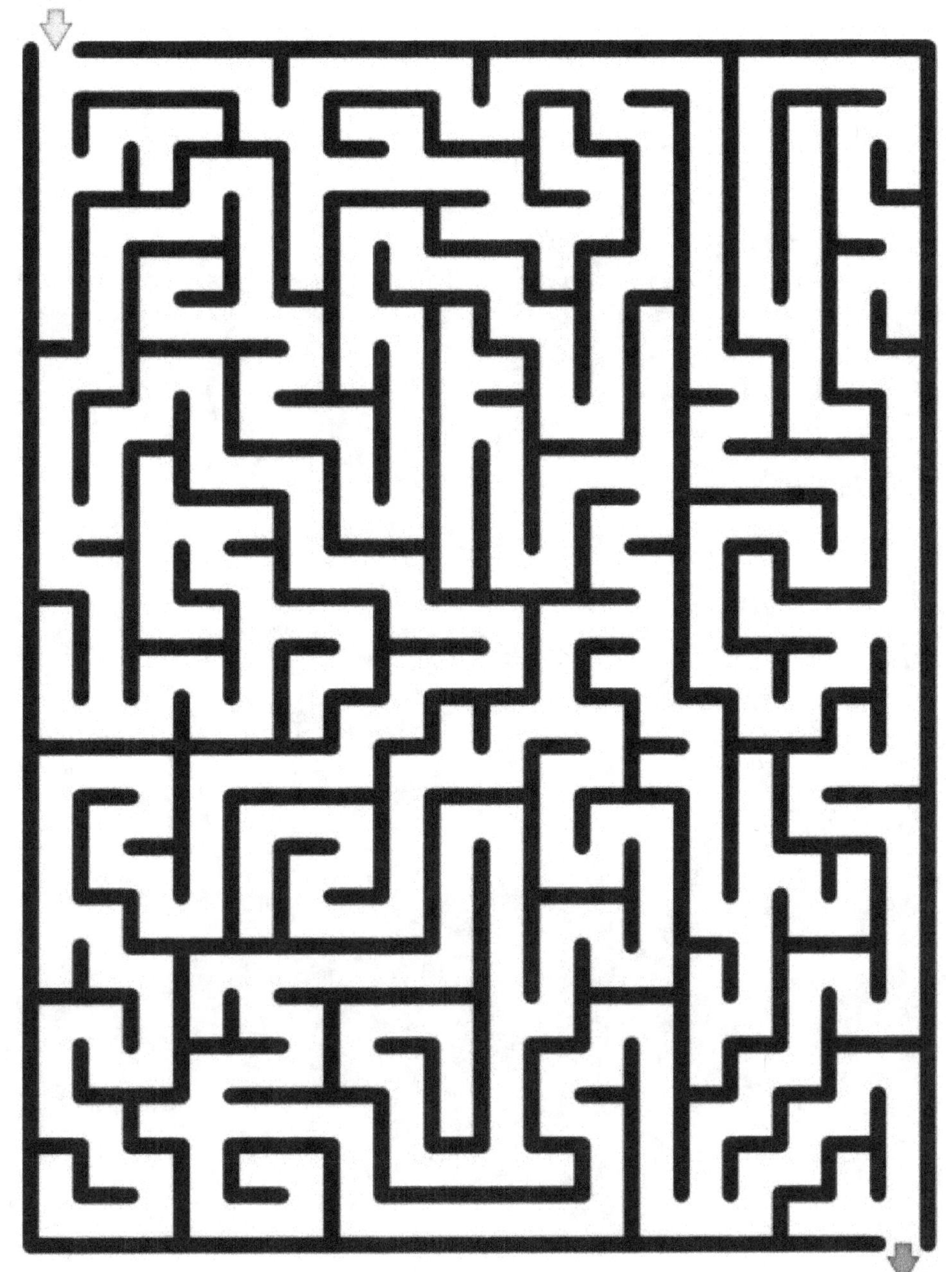

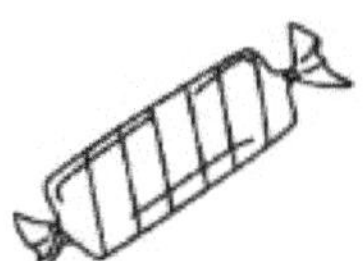

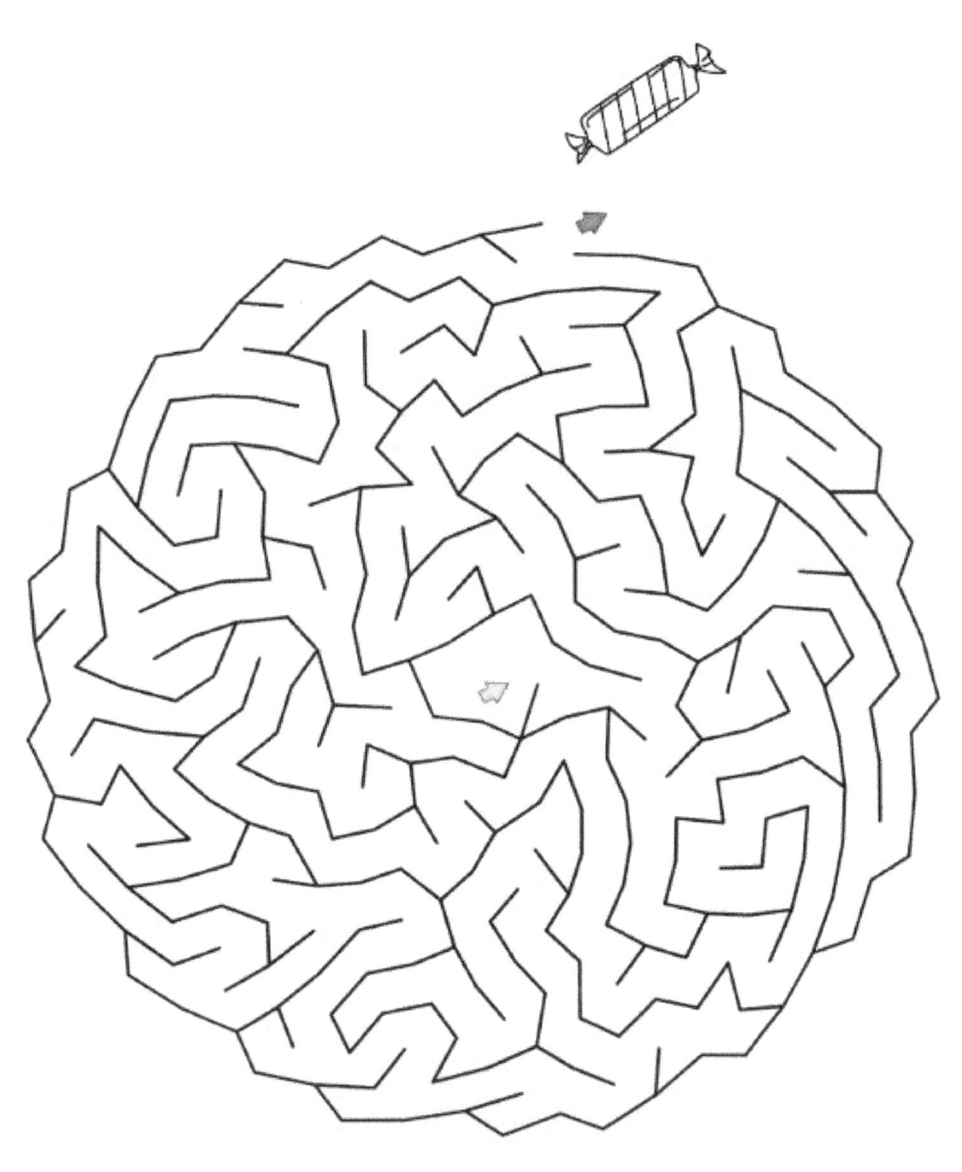

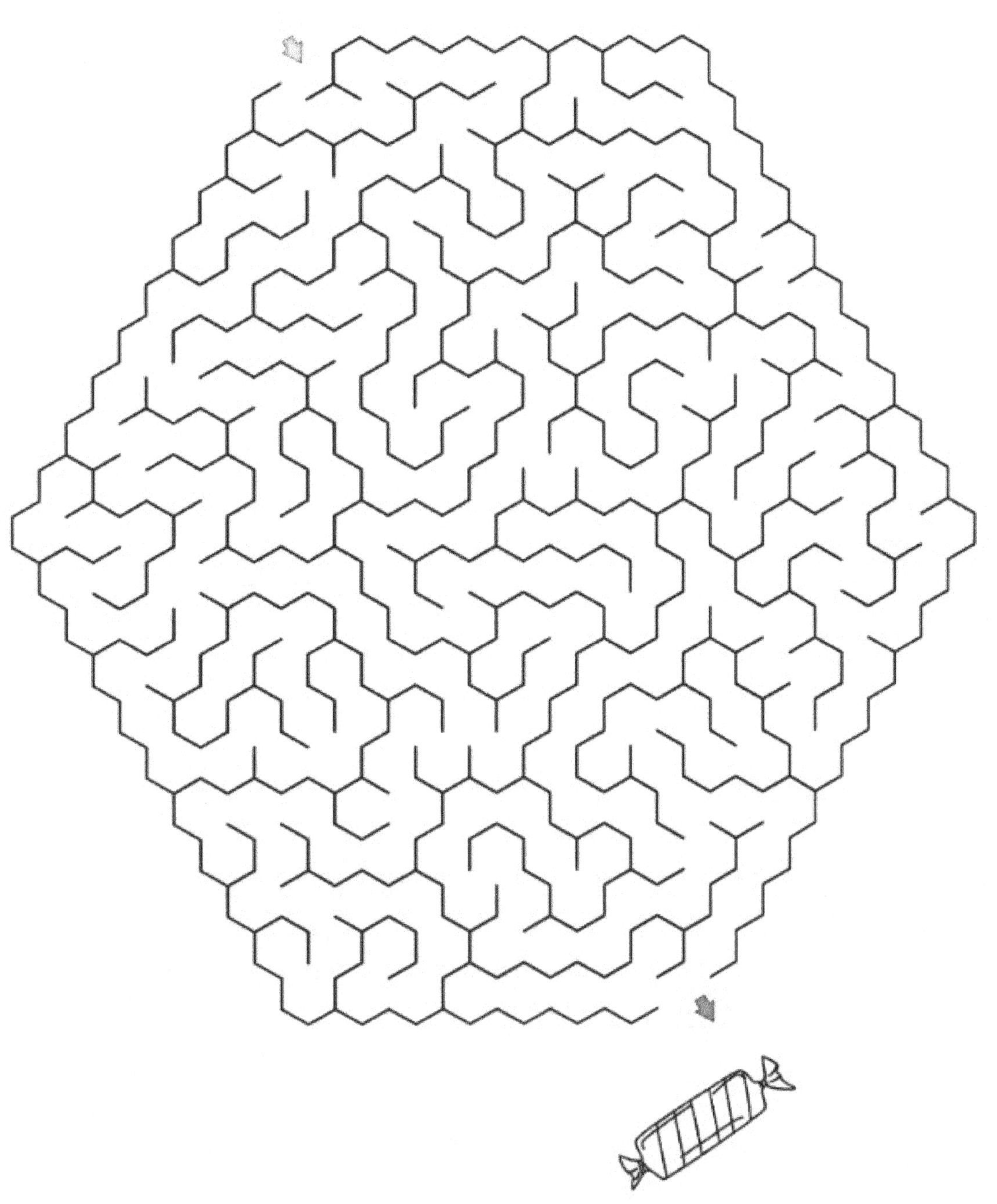

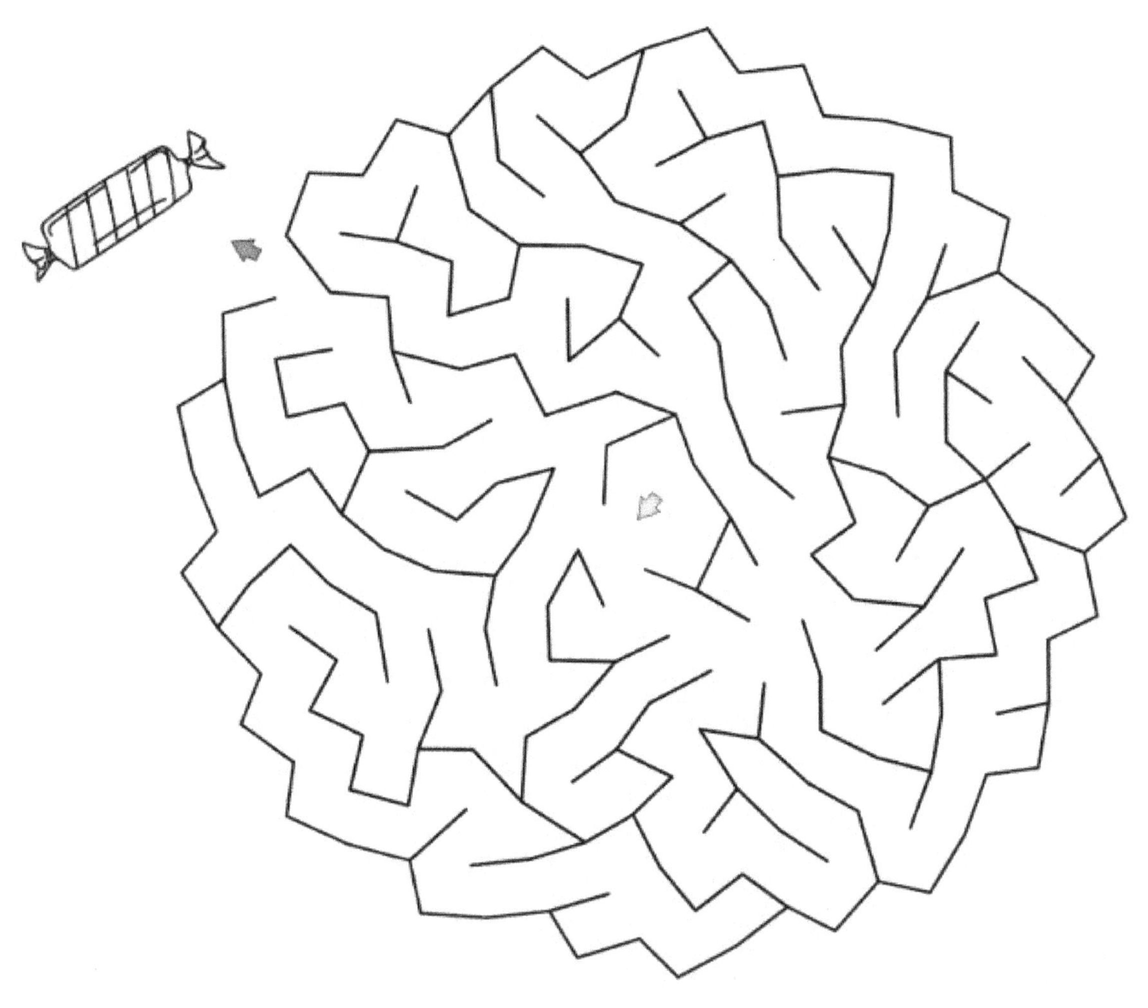

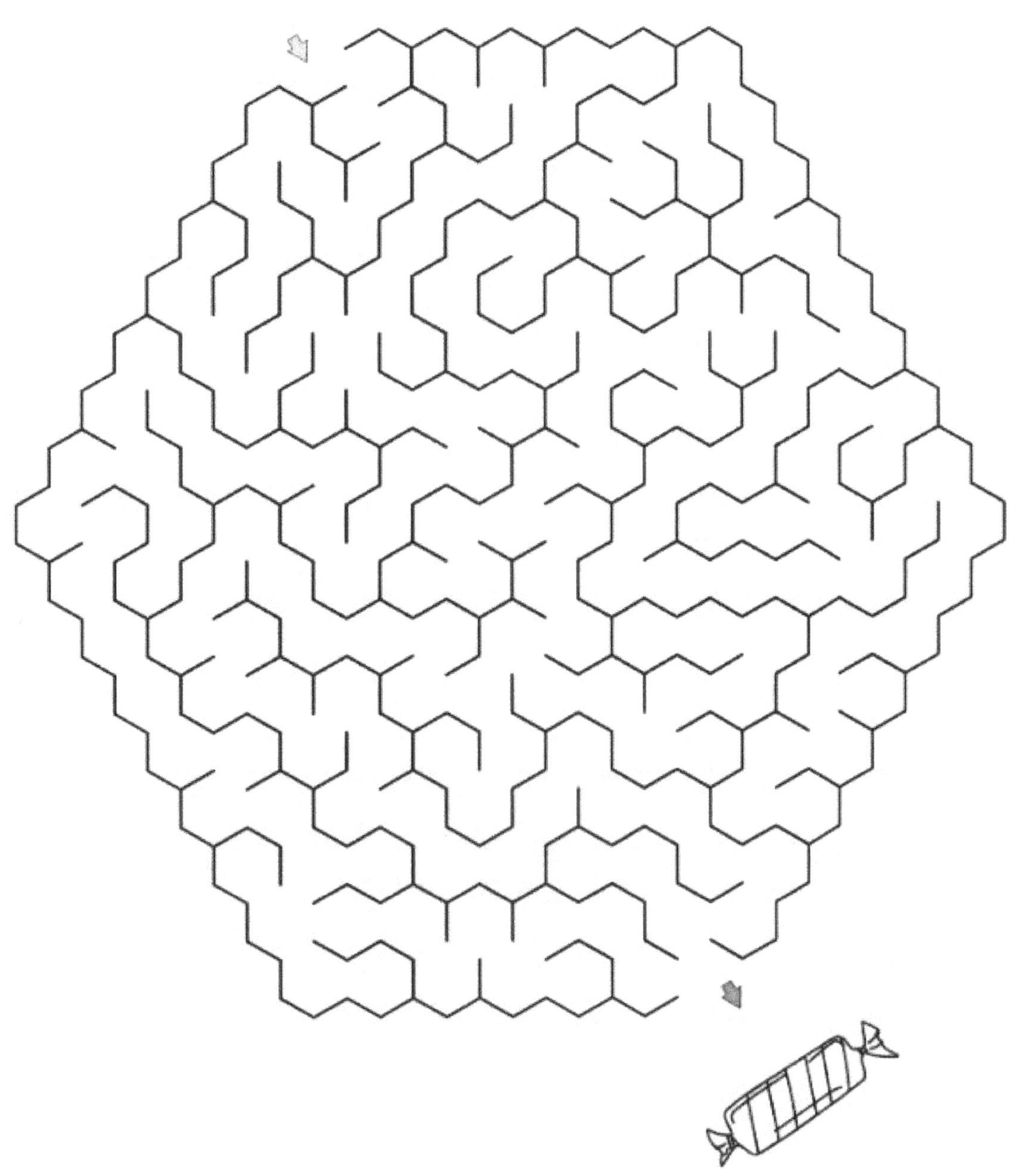

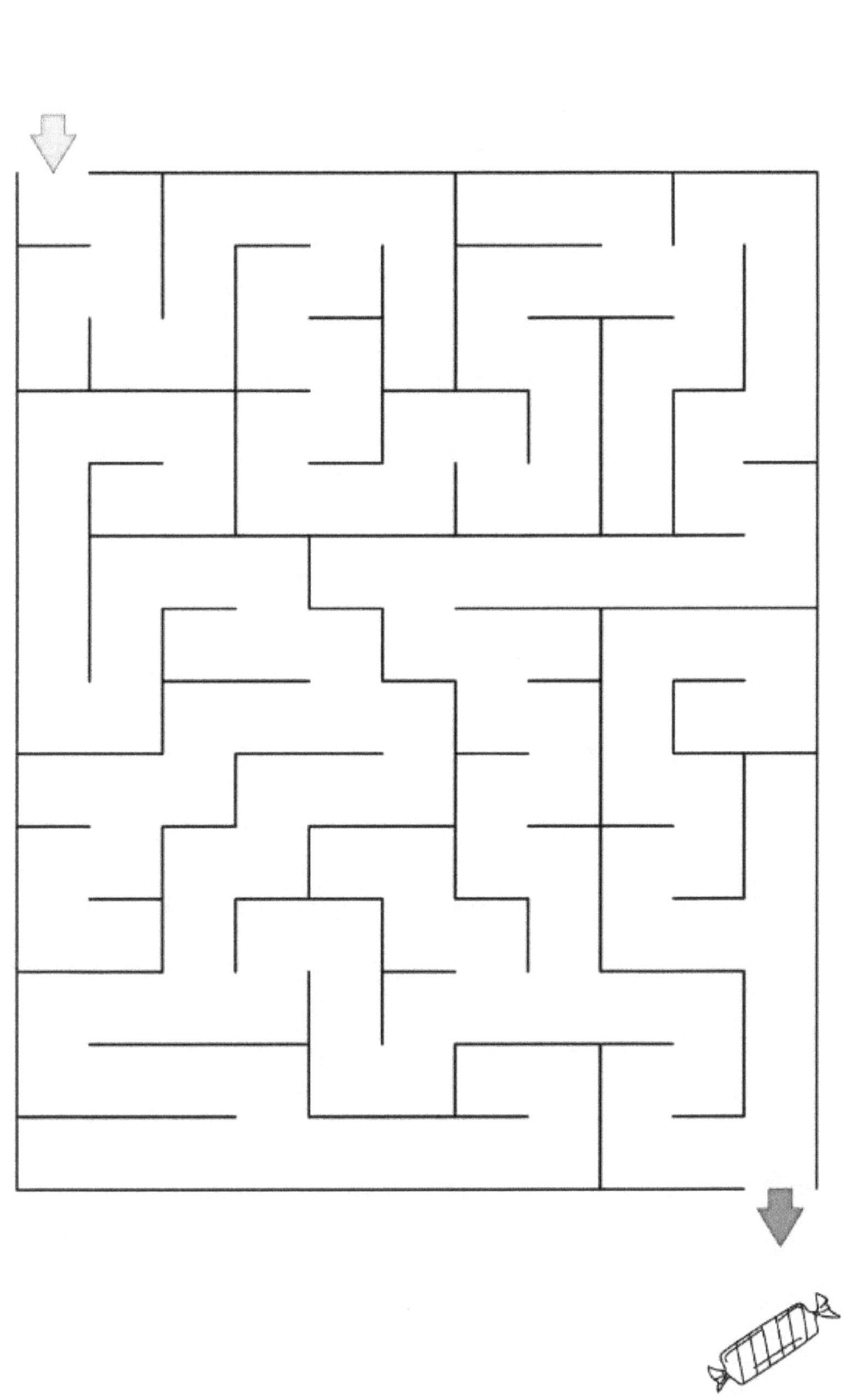

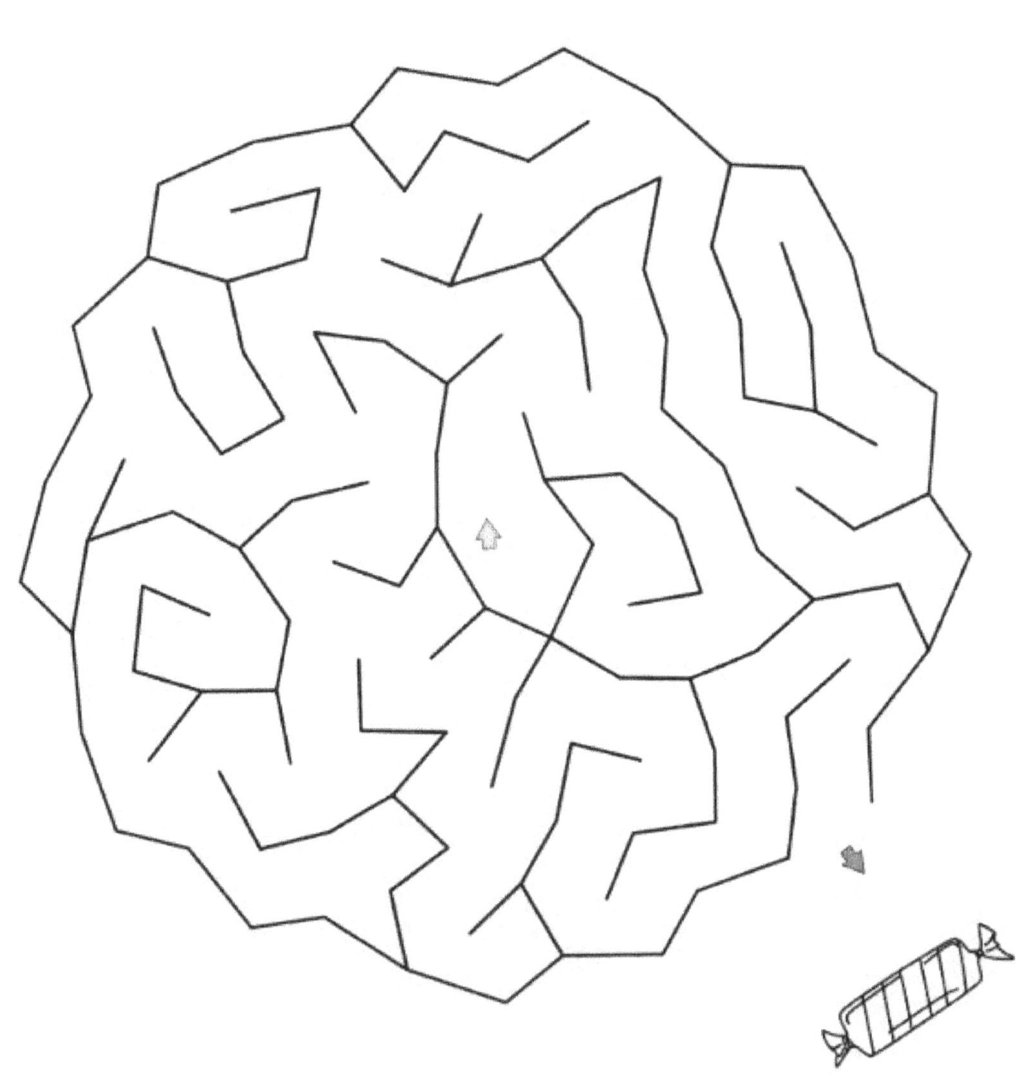

www.ingramcontent.com/pod-product-compliance
Lightning Source LLC
Chambersburg PA
CBHW081737250726
48657CB00010B/3314